The List of Last Tries

Jessica L. Walsh

Cover and interior design by Sable Books

ISBN 978-0-9987810-7-5

Sable Books
sablebooks.org

Contents

In the Trees a Retreat

She was so disagreeable that eventually she was expelled from her village. When she arrived at another village the people there asked her, 'Why did you leave your home?' She replied, 'Oh, all the people in that village were wicked; I left in order to escape from them.' The people thought it odd that a whole village should be so bad, and concluded that it was the old lady herself who was at fault. Fearing that she would cause them nothing but trouble, they threw her out of their village as well.

—*How to Solve Our Human Problems,*
Geshe Kelsang Gyatso

for unpleasant women,
that we may be our own village

So Say They All

At Birth, A Human Form

I come with a shaking shadow

fatten myself on night walks
and dark porch corners.

Some days I scoff at them
   not reject but recluse.
Perhaps snob
more often pariah

      whether dodgeball or chem lab

      walking to or from

forcibly alone

as though around me hovers
 putrid clouds.

I run circles
centrifuge
      mix and separate

but somehow return to form
the woman
 who drinks light
  and small blessings.

Self Portrait as Spilled Milk

Not to be cried over
but cleaned up.

Accidents,
my mother said,
are not without consequence.

She tried her hardest
on everyday messes:
   scrubbed at stains
    while saving grocery money
      for slipcovers;

   relegated too-damaged rugs
    to a bedroom
    where company wouldn't see.

Though she kept my clothes starched,
  my mouth closed to starches,
I stayed a stain
impossible to cover.

When company came
I went to my room.

Bitter

On my list of last tries:
summer camp

where soon they know me
as enemy, as effigy.

The pretty girl
who brought pink and purple pens
and pictures of boy bands
finds a fat brown bug on her pillow case.

She shrieks *Gross*
as required by popular girls

shakes the bug to the floor
where it twitches on its back.

My brother said you can eat those
another girl squeals.

I do not care for the bug
but the girls are worse.

I dare them to fear
as I squat to pluck it off the planks,
    stand straight
        and swallow it.

And if I say how it tastes
or how the air feels
in the ring of untouching
that forms around me?

That too is bitter.

Will Not Respond to Reason

Even my boots
I pack with food:
     hard candies and crab cakes,
     shelf stable stuffed among spoiling
but no matter,
eating is never my goal.

I won't starve
but I want someone to.

When the flies thicken at my door
my mother arrives to weep
over marvelous rotting heaps,
my father to rasp
  What a waste.

Within hours
they resume
not seeing.

The Pretender

The ruddy black-haired one
in the silver frame beside my mother
looks past the camera,
maybe conjuring a portal
or signaling for gin—

and the gaunt one in the living room
  whose chair seems a corduroy parasite
  fattening its cushions around him
  as his thinning bones scrape
  through a day of not dying—

impossible they are the same.
Time alone cannot account.

But she speaks as though they are one man.

Each morning the pretender stares
at a hardboiled egg
served to him on a tv tray.

My mother once told me his first job
was egg candler,
holding shells to light
  seeking out unwanted bodies
  and tossing them into a bucket labeled PIG—

like holding a paper doll
against a sun-cut window
  seeing a tiny heart beating
and feeding it all to a shredder,

like finding under a scarecrow's torn shirt
a tangle of gentle human guts
and burning him at his stake.

The consequence of nearly living
has always been death.

He will hear you, she says.
You are killing your father.

Expiration Date

That evening we see he has died
unremarkably and still.
We carry his hollow-boned body
from the brown carapace of his chair
to the bed where I was born.

My mother's sighs lengthen,
her lungs sending forth roomfuls of air.

She sits on the edge of the bed
and looks up towards my eyes,
begins patting her hair
and smoothing her eyebrows
like I hold a mirror showing her flaws.

I am sorry about your birthday, she says,
touching the edge of her mouth.
He wanted to see you grown.

That night in bed beside him
her heart stops
on schedule.

She will guide him through
one more world
he will not understand.

The undertaker
  unshaven at that hour
takes my hand. He soothes
So devoted to family—
they lived only for you, dear.

I was their sentence,
the time they had to serve.

Spine straight for judgment
I sit on the sofa's edge
long after he has taken them.

Morning inches upwards.
Sunlight drenches the living room
and our thirsty dust strains to drink its rays.

On the fireplace mantle
the woodgrain's dark lines glint
like a tally marking
my six thousand days.

Vivisection

Unpartnered at school
I dissect alone

split worms lengthwise
pop open cow eyes
  aqueous and vitreous
both viscous
  on old pages of the Daily News.

In my cornea obituaries bulge
  and fog.

When it comes to hearts the teacher has only one,
cut from fall's first kill
as most bucks still roam the woods.

We line the table to watch
and classmates lean over me to see
as he names valves and chambers.

When his heart is exhausted
he brings out a coffee can of bacon fat
and an electric skillet
where he fries up the heart
              now turned venison.
He serves it with crackers and cheese.

Everyone chews and swallows
even those who gag.

I know the crackers
as the brand I once stole from the drugstore.
When she found out, she said
      nothing
but one more word appeared
  on the list of forbiddens.

How pleasant
to taste them again,
even under game and sweating cheese
in a scalpeled room
where I stand apart.

To Town with My Body

I walk without cadence,
lacking lovely one-inch heels just ahead of me
to set pace and path.

Unleashed from the hem of my mother's dress
I meet the eyes of the townsfolk.

Their faces bear messages
in an alphabet I can't read.

What do they mean
in their measured manners?

Which twitches spell out greetings?
Which signal warnings?

What is the face for pity
and what means fear?

I sour with no translator,
guessing the wordless nod
  or doorway yield
are purposeful abrasions,
part of the process
of tanning my hide to translucence
    preparing me to be thin-skinned.

No cause to see kindness.

Block Party

Spring comes months after,
when I am firmly a woman on earth
who no longer has people.

I was determined not to try
but I admit I fail on this
the last Sunday.

I come down the pocked walk
in a clean dress—

> past the mailbox bearing most of our name
> but for a bullet hole through one letter
> long since rusted.

My hair brushed nearly straight,
I stand with my arms at my sides:
posture.

All the soft-shouldered folk who shuffled past me
on the day of the funerals,
their feet dragging on plush chapel rugs
now stand clustered on plush lawns,
their eyes skittering over me
like the line of a radar
as it chirps out the shape and place
of what could be a problem.
No one approaches.

I wanted little: to tell a story
and keep parts of it to myself.
Instead I stand beside the crystal punchbowl set
and everyone goes thirsty.

The Eyesore, The Nuisance

In the absence of parents
weeds seize the yard.

Grass gives way to grass-like,
green to another palette of green.

The papery jittery moths
and hooting mourning doves

are far indeed from
monarchs and finches,

but neither are they swarming bees
and rabid bats.

The village sends warnings
and I pretend not to read them.

When I receive a fine, I pay it,
then watch the weeds grow thicker.

Embryonic

In the years before my father sat down
he walked dawn's yard daily
murmuring names of birds
I could hear if I crept close and silent
  to the edge of the back porch.

His handkerchief cradled seed for them
  or scraps of sweets my mother baked and forbade.

Sometimes a crow
  unadmired like me
left junk
  shiny bottle caps
  shards of glass
  a clothespin from a house in the magic land
    where women hugged children into their aprons.

Today I crack an egg
into the cast iron skillet
  brought west in a wagon
    by an unremembered ancestor
spiteful enough to settle here

and a bloody would-be chicken
  slides fast across the pan
its wings aspiring and unfinished
  beak too large
    eyes too small.

Nothing to eat or cherish.

I walk the yard alone
but whenever they see me
  birds call fear
    dart to neighbors' trees

our branches going slowly to bone
above the impassable feral.

Little Children, Never Linger

On the last day of my schooling
the teacher backs away from me:
What you want is always on your face.

  Little children never linger,
  close your eyes tight, turn your head.

I never threw or chased
never stalked or shrieked
but kids arc wide around me.

  Both her parents died right by her
  while she slept all night in bed.

I am hardly grown
and already legend.

  Little children, never linger!
  Stay away, like mother said--

From a dark porch corner
I listen for the nursery rhyme
that sings the story of
what is on my face.

  If she points her bony finger
  you're the next to fall down dead.

Births and Deaths

The spine breaks
when I open *Poems for Every Occasion*;
pages flake
as I drag my net
for words to work
like a knife at their necks
   or my own
on this, the occasion of my surrender.
But poets can't finish without mercy—
their blades come blessed
or dulled with rust of ancestors
  who'd hacked free.

No poems for a woman
deadly/alone
ready to announce herself
all she has been called:
freak witch murderer curse.

I thump the book into the fireplace
then reach for my father's old newspapers
neatly stacked beside logs.

In kindling,
the words I need--
every page hisses
of a child left to starve,
a war machine mistake,
a family killed en route to church,
rendered in merciless fact.

Journalists run with dirty razors
and I join them:
I try for sepsis
and visible scars,
all harm intentional.

Department of Public Works

The city water man comes to do it
his voice muffled
head dropped below shoulders
as he hunches down
between molded wall and spidery furnace
to read the meter. *Fine place,* he says.
*Folks been asking if you're staying
or if you got people somewhere.
It's a lot for a girl, huh?*

He scratches numbers on a dirty notepad,
not expecting a response.

Tucking away pencil and paper,
he pats pockets for belongings
then points to the bathroom: *Can I?*

I say no, I admit, gleefully.

He wipes his hands on his pants.
*See, now, that's what I mean.
I mean, suit yourself...*
and he squirms through his own nonsense.

That is how they drive me out:
the town sends a meter man
and all his broken sentences
to tell me what they would never dream of saying.
You are what's wrong.

The Second Quarantine

Fallow Season

I burn to dirt
then relight my own hotspots
until gray remains alone
like cigarette ash.

I lie cooling a moon
and the next,
suspend myself
while no one waits.

I collect myself
on a misted morning,
its horizon lost to fog.
Dogs sleep on porches
twitching through dreams
of beasts unnamed
to be played with or preyed upon,
depending on the first move.

Legend of My New Beginning

I can afford tired places.

My second town ate itself into being
fattening on lumber
until no trees stood.

After wood came copper
then corrosives
now mostly not much
except hunting season
and a deal to frack
if the land has anything in it.

The whole place is what it used to be:
old pharmacy where they sold hot peanuts
old grocery store and the place above the old grocery store
old Jorgenson farm at the corner by the old highway.
Livvie's old newsstand
sells flowers now.

Things are found
where lost things were.

Even the town itself
was another town
long gone to the dam.

At the lake, beams of underwater town
are fishermen's bearings.

What was here, I ask
from the edge of the front walk
looking to a door on the second floor
that opens only to air.
The landlord shrugs,
Oh, lots of things.
And with no better choices
I move in
unsure where I live
and how to find my way.

These Must Be Your Beasts

The new place comes with cats
scraps of ratty feral fur on mange
darting garden to garbage.

The man next door flicks his eyes
from me to them and back again.
He prepares to hate me if I feed our strays,
growing their sour mess.

And when I do not—
   when I let the cats wail and linger
slowly wasting to wormy street cat weight—
he hates me for that.

He never tells me his name
or asks mine
doesn't ask his wife to drop by with bread.
Our yards touch at hunger.

Only once he speaks
to say he's called animal control
to kill them
and a cruelty hotline
to save them.
Either way.

A woman like me makes sense with cats.
On that we'd likely agree.

Furniture Candy Groceries Chrome

A sign in three fonts,
furniture and *chrome* flaking away
in chips of paint and rust.

I try to imagine the town with money,
locals buying furniture
or caring for treasured cars.
Surely those were short-lived days.

Maybe these people grew up like me:
you're supposed to do better/
you'll never do better.

But if in my gut I string a rope bridge
hoping someone could cross,

the owner wastes no time in cutting it down
when I empty my basket
onto the chipped laminate counter.

Each item a judgment
and a question he's already answered
in quiet front-porch gossip
that traveled before me:

Usually it's older folks pick that one.

You looking to join the garden club?
It's a nice thing for the ladies.
You don't seem the type, though.

Never seen a woman buy that!
Have a young man coming to visit?

To each his own,
he says,
and that means its opposite.

Cataloging

Though I've memorized taxonomies
    taxidermy: 579 / QL63
    tachometry: 629 / TL152
the librarian will not have me—

she knows I'll be a child-shusher,
an eye-rolling antagonist of the genealogists,
an angry aisle witch.
No, thank you, it's not a good fit.

I circle my finger on the counter between us
to form a screen for memory
and play for her my girlhood
grazing stacks
wandering the pasture of shadowed shelves
away from reflection.

When the scene ends
her eyebrows undulate
as she flips through expressions.
She takes half a step back.

I dream of breaking in: of daybreak
when they find a shelving perfection,
spines all flush and unsmudged,
collections immaculate.

Like classmates,
they claim my work as their own
even as they glance around
to be sure I am gone.

Unredeemable

On green days I still look up,
connect my eyes with another's,
tantalized.

In Tartarus I think
Tantalus suffered nor hunger nor thirst
but ever-replenishing hope.

Pity him,
believing he could beat
whatever strange machine
the gods crafted
if he reached out one more time.

I dream only of not wanting
of standing perfect in my misery.

Straight

Behind my house
train tracks break towards forest,
   the only traffic
   skinny folk walking fast.

Surely a shed lurks in the woods
   built for syrup or hunting
now a rustbelt cookhouse
getting folks through.

I would follow rails
   to a slower house
if I ever earned my poison.

My receptors are sockets
for the morphine plug.

I could cut my way to methadone,
oxy, cheap black tar.

But my mind's machines
run on hunger.

I stay straight
because I deserve
life unrelieved.

Canopy Bed

My parents claimed the trees were wrong
and couldn't hold

but I'd sketched anyway:
a treehouse, a hunting blind

above and among
inscrutable faces.

My parents lied about the strength of trees
and childhood.

I approve of their lie,
how it built a space
for their cruelty
stretched across the grove of oak.

Here a brittle elm
too sick to hold.

Your Future for a Fee

Unwashing years
glaze windows. Private
and invisible,

I work from home
as professional hag
weird sister
mail order banshee.

Doomed humans believe
I speak the language of stars
and pay for my warnings.
Month to month
I oracle.

With files and maps,
I scream deadly prophecies:

> Folks, you'll suffer
> as I have.
> Someone has to.

I eat off dread.

What I Eat Dirty

Whatever is underneath my fingernails
    when I am tired and trembling.

A grandfather's lemon drops
    found wedged under the edge
of the ancient pea-green rug
    covering the perfect oak floors.

My cuticles.

Olives abandoned in anyone's glasses
        when the lights go on at 1:53
 peoples' startled eyes on me
as though I can only be seen fluorescent.

Icicles I knock down with a broom
        then dig from the earth-grey snow.

The last page of the last paper letter
        describing what they wanted me to be.

The skin of my cracking mouth.

Night Garden

I grow tomatoes
to lure midnight worms.

I assign black hours to watching.

At the right line of colorless dark
the faceless stumps of fat creep out

legs mere bumps on bellies
bellies dragging through dirt.

They overeat. They eat themselves taut
and still they eat.

The tomatoes ungrow
aborted by the worms I call forth,
and still I call.

My legs ungrow
drained and scathed
by ticks who come to my pested feast
and find me splayed for tasting.

Before dawn before green
before worms retreat
I knife around my fat full ticks
and throw the tiny chunks toward garden.

I pick my scars.

The Enemy's Present

At yard's edge
        neither lawn nor alley
grass and gravel
share space.

The land's unbeing
draws garbage to it
  cans bags cigarette butts
a ribbon of litter.

Confusion exhausts me.

From the neighbor's shed
I steal a spade
and make a thick dirt line:

Here wild begins   and here tame.
I tend the border.

When frost calls for edges
he comes for his spade,
sits across from me
at the kitchen table
pretending his chair doesn't wobble.

He tries to be polite but
as the boiler gutters awake
in my pipe-veined basement
I tell him it's mine now

and he pronounces me foe,
says everyone was right.

His chair scrapes the floor
as he stands to leave
but I stay in my place.

Every Town a Tooth

At a strange hour I break a tooth
grinding my dream-angry jaw.

I wait for day
for dentist
to pull it clean out
and offer it back to me
in a plastic cup.

That night-gone-morning
I remember my Sunday school teacher
in her tranquil pastel cardigan
and as she talked of forgiveness
she seemed sedated but claimed grace.
Her voice floated easy and even
like she was deciding on brunch
or where to place pillows in a cottage.

Did they seek forgiveness
    my parents   neighbors   towns?
Was I out of earshot?

                I lick my broken tooth
                    marking minutes with strings of pain.

Down the Back of My Throat

Dilute your anger in a tranquil sea,
the social worker says, acting the smug hermit
who feared no mirror.

Fifty minutes later he confesses
his advice is useless
for the poison that cures in my teeth.

My toxins are spectacular,
like none he's seen,
the kind no ocean can take.

He foresees the fish kill—
the dead shining across the water
and me a revelation of venom.

My closed mouth is pardon
for him and the beasts of the seas.
If anger is all I have, I'll drink it.

Then Again the Rats

Dead animals
congest my threshold.

I would be goddess,
declare them sacrifices made in fearful awe
offerings on the steps of my temple,
fresh-caught flesh beseeching blessing.

But what they bring
even if wishful

all rots   draws flies
forms a rancid pool.

The mess is mortal
and not mine to clean.

In the Trees a Retreat

Capacity

Exceeding the maximum weight
one woman carries,
a competent life
splits into symmetrical halves
that meet at high noon
day after day
until the only remembered thing
is that the other must be killed
before lunch.

Imagine for a moment
I am not the problem,
not at first.

Getting Dressed

I weary of wardrobe changes.

My body rings trash
in all towns.

I am never mistaken
for a body with a cottage
and a hobby.

I toss out their pamphlets:
       Nutrition on a Budget
       Facts About Sleep.

My body holds broke and country
no matter its costume.

Lede

By day I sort possessions—
    destroy, abandon, burn—

and at night I set metal letters
backwards   ready for printing

> Postal Service Investigates Person Leaving Meat,
>   Maggots in Mailboxes

> and

> Shopper on Rampage Breaks Entire Stock of Eggs

But wet from the press
in endless reprintings
the page reads

Police: No Reason to Investigate Missing Woman

Go Ahead and Go Away

I turn the deadbolt behind me
but leave keys hanging in the lock.

What have they wanted
more than this—
my walking away,
skull braced for thrown stones?

Their judgment muscular
but arms weak,
they let me pass.

Sidewalks break behind me
and from cracks in the concrete
rotten water bubbles up
to wash away my scent.

Thirty Days Past Due

After a reasonable month
    a full billing cycle after all
and the lawn gone to wild yet again

the curious men will come—
a deputy, the landlord,
his handkerchief ready
in case the scene is grim

but they'll find nobody dead or sick
No body.

A house unpeopled.
The best outcome.

In my room
I left my clothes on the bed
cut in half
from top to bottom
arranged in two symmetrical piles.

Useful wives will sew
halves back to whole

and chafing at the stitches
they'll stay apart from others
unsure at what distance
the seams can be seen.

Hope for Haunted

Ill-equipped to picture my rooms
alive with children laughing past bedtime
or artists washing glass
for unfiltered sun

I choose bruised stories,
alienation's aftermath.

I dream of houses gone hollow,
windows broken by timid kids
  afraid to go further.

Imagine my legacy
as malignant land
and nightmares.

Nest of Bones

No need for eagles
when I can claw my own liver,
scatter it to the stones below
for scavengers that scurry forth
while I close my eyes against
the hot work of reproducing guts I give away.

Even songbirds turn carnivorous.
Yellow finches red-beak into
skunk guts abandoned to rot.

Photosynthetic hunger strike,
these twigs like twigs
pecked into a nest
laced with bones from wings and fingers
            white to the sky
                louseless past maggots.

The wild allures   murders
disposes of loose bones
repeats a measure of song for mating.

Eggs might come of this
my long lost limb.

Time Unbiased

I lack tools   food
a plan for winter
in this my last home
  a zone of expulsions.

Birds sing the same at dawn
for tangled lovers and crumpled victims,
even for me, nearly gone
in a mix of childhood and anger,

trying to hear in their melody
a sign for where I will go next.

After Gravity

You will find me
in a house
    that undoes itself
        its nails easing
        from wood
    dated landscapes
drifting out windows
    rugs aspiring to flight
        mop expanding
beyond its bucket
        the water parting
            into drops
                each a dirty universe
                glimmering skyward
carrying with it all the earthly wrongs.

I can't hold my hands up forever.

Acknowledgments

I thank the tough and difficult ancestors who preceded me; my daughter who carries us into the future; my husband, the man who lived; my tender and fierce family; Jenn Givhan, for her input and guidance; Melissa Hassard, for her meticulous and inspired editorial vision; my village of writers and believers.

I extend my gratitude to *White Stag, Tinderbox, Sundog, North Dakota Review, Midwestern Gothic, Little River, The Fem, Whale Road, Yellow Chair Review, TRIVIA: Voices of Feminism, Great Lakes Review* and *The Connecticut River Review* for publishing poems that appear in this volume. Additional poems were originally published in draft form as part of the *Tupelo Press 30/30 Project* for September 2014.

Praise for This Collection

Unapologetic, unrepentant, wild-as-weeds and willing to swallow any bitter insect on a dare, to eat whatever crawls beneath her fingernails, Jessica Walsh's girl-turned-woman speaker is refreshingly "impassable feral," and her *List of Last Tries* sings her ballad, a battle cry, a fable for our times. And at its center is a woman who doesn't seek redemption, won't apologize for her unsmiling, her letting the stray neighborhood cats "waste to wormy street cat weight," won't pull the weeds, "will not respond to reason," and refuses to play along to any "meter man" the town may send with "all his broken sentences." In a time where the literary world condemns our unlikable characters and politicians tell us to get our coat hangers ready, Walsh responds with a powerful girl/woman indeed: "a woman / deadly/alone / ready to announce herself / all she has been called: / freak witch murderer curse." The startling, haunting, and empowering world of Walsh's collection is "like holding a paper doll / against a sun-cut window / seeing a tiny heart beating / and feeding it all to a shredder"—dark and engaging, this collection upholds storytelling as the ultimate truth, and even then, a woman can withhold as a sign of her own strength, as Walsh well knows: "I wanted little: to tell a story / and keep parts of it to myself."

— Jenn Givhan, *Landscape with Headless Mama, Girl with Death Mask*

Jessica Walsh's *The List of Last Tries* is a miracle of focus, a sustained gothic nursery rhyme that describes a girl's coming of age and coming into power, for which she is shunned and exiled as freak, witch, and murderer. She "split(s) worms lengthwise," "pop(s) open cow eyes," and even eats a bug in defiance of the conventional shrieks of other girls. Her mother "sav(es) grocery money for slipcovers" but our girl is an unmaskable stain, a paper doll with a beating heart fed to the shredder. Later, when she is "a woman without people" in another town, she makes her living "as professional hag"—"I oracle," she writes—and tends the border between wild and tame. List of Last Tries is a captivating female picaresque, each poem taking a step deeper into marginality's fierce power. When Walsh's speaker breaks the spine of

Poems for Every Occasion and, finding nothing to help her there, burns it, she does what witches do—she concocts her own volume of myths and enchantments. The result is the book that you are holding in your hands.

— Diane Seuss, *Still Life with Two Dead Peacocks and a Girl, Four- Legged Girl*, Pulitzer Prize Finalist

Jessica Walsh's *The List of Last Tries* embodies the uncanny seamlessly, unnervingly, and with delightful swagger. The body anchoring these poems is defiantly female; the speaker is feminine on her own enraged, macabre, fearless terms. She amplifies her awkwardness, anxiety, interpersonal missteps, abandonment, and solitude in order to weaponize them against anyone who would stand too close for the wrong reasons. This is a consciousness that offers unwavering scrutiny through the dissection of animal organs; who determinedly cultivates species of invasive weeds, while a tenacious sense of inertia builds into something like power; and who pauses to note, pleasantly, how half-melted dairy enhances the chilling indulgence of consuming a recently-beating heart. This book opens again and again like an unlit doorway in front of you, and the presence floating inside dares you to walk through it. Walk through it.

— Fox Frazier-Foley, *The Hyrdromantic Histories* and *Like Ash in the Air After Something Has Burned*

9780998781075